Leonardo

Leonardo

Arnoldo Mondadori Arte

Texts by Roberta Villa

Translation by David Stanton

Table of Contents

Leonardo

The age in which Leonardo lived was certainly one of the most stimulating and one of the richest in innovatory and creative ferment. After the rebirth of the humanities and the revival of the arts in the period from 1450 to 1550, man, now the "centre of the world," was able to greatly widen the horizons of his knowledge. The invention of the printing press, an invaluable means of diffusing culture, and the discovery of new continents and civilisations were only two aspects of that remarkable period of history in which Leonardo da Vinci lived and worked. His extremely versatile mind ranged over every possible area of science, technology and art, searching in every field for the common mechanisms and fundamental laws which govern and create natural phenomena.

Almost nothing is known about the early activity of Leonardo, who was born in 1452 near Vinci, a small town not far from Florence. The Florentine artistic milieu, and in particular the workshop of Andrea Verrocchio, where between about 1469 and 1478 he served his first apprenticeship, were of fundamental importance for his later activity. His artistic education with his talented master—who was painter, sculptor, goldsmith and musician—and the continuous exchange of ideas with his fellow pupils, instilled in him a modern concept of art. This was no longer a mechanical imitation of nature, but rather a way of discovering it through scientific understanding of its laws, rationally reproduced in the work of art through the application of the newly invented rules of perspective.

In Milan, where he lived from 1482 to 1499, inspired by the circle of literati, artists and scientists who gravitated towards the court of Ludovico il Moro, he threw himself with ever-growing passion into the study of mathematics, anatomy, mechanics, optics, hydraulics and botany. The paintings he executed in Milan show the close links that existed between his scientific and artistic research, which for Leonardo were activities that complemented each other perfectly. In the years after he left Milan, which he spent in Florence, Milan again and Rome, Leonardo's interests grew in an eclectic fashion, and he expressed them through inventions, plans, drawings and notes on a great variety of topics. Nevertheless, he continued to dedicate himself to painting, which he considered to be the highest form of artistic expression. It is significant that he kept with him during the years he spent in France (1516-1519), until his death, the work which was the high point of his artistic and scientific research, a painting which has always been recognised as one of the great masterpieces of all time, the *Mona Lisa* (Plates 35, 36), which not long ago was defined as "the painted autobiography of the artist."

The Florentine Period (1452-1482)

It is quite surprising to discover that the amount of certain biographical information regarding Leonardo is extremely limited. Despite the enormous quantity of manuscripts and drawings which have remained as a precious inheritance, contemporary accounts are few and far between, there are not many letters and only a handful of drawings and paintings can be dated with certainty. It is, therefore, not possible to find out much about his adolescent years and it is a very arduous task to try to piece together the early stages of his artistic education.

Illegitimate child of a notary called Pietro d'Antonio and a certain Caterina, Leonardo was born near Vinci on 15 April 1452. In 1469 his father moved with the family to Florence, where he had been appointed notary of the Signoria, the republican government of the city. Leonardo, who was then seventeen years old, was admitted to the workshop of Andrea Verrocchio, where he found himself in the company of such budding young artists as Domenico Ghirlandaio, Pietro Perugino, Sandro Botticelli and Lorenzo di Credi. He remained there for about eight years, at first absorbing the basic achievements of the Florentine Renaissance, learning from his master greater fluency in composition, and then, following his own natural disposition, rebelling against the intellectual rigidity, the linear style and the harshness of form which was typical of much Florentine painting in the second half of the Quattrocento. The young Leonardo quickly learned the value of first-hand experience, hence the direct observation of natural phenomena came to be of prime importance in the process of his artistic development. Consequently the break with the Florentine art world, which at that time was influenced by the vaguely spiritu-

alising aestheticism of the Neo-Platonics was inevitable. In fact, in 1482 Leonardo left Florence for Milan, placing his skills at the disposal of the Sforza family.

It is generally extremely difficult to establish the precise responsibility of Leonardo for the paintings produced by Verrocchio's workshop, given the way the work was organised, which required close collaboration between the pupils. On the other hand, there can be no doubt regarding the drawing of the *Arno Landscape* (Plate 1) in the Uffizi, the first work to be dated by Leonardo, on the basis of an inscription in his hand with the date 5 August 1473.

A year after his enrolment in the painters' guild—which confirmed his virtual independence from Verrocchio and, as a consequence, the acquisition of the right to receive commissions himself—in the Uffizi drawing the artist displayed a new way of looking at nature. The world was exactly as it appeared to him, with the atmosphere no longer perfectly transparent, but forming a filter between the sight and the image, thus changing visual perception. The forms of the distant landscape are no longer distinct, but they seem to vibrate due to the volatility of the atmosphere, with its almost tangible air and light. The drawing, executed by the artist at the age of twenty-one, already foreshadowed the interest, which he then continued to develop for the rest of his life, in natural phenomena and his concept of art as a means of investigating these.

Moreover the first sample of the young Leonardo's painting skills generally recognised by scholars fully confirms this disposition. The child-like face of the angel on the left of Verrocchio's *Baptism of Christ* (Plates 2, 3) is modelled with extremely delicate gradations of colour. The lineaments seem to dissolve due to the light which softens the outlines, but which at the same time gives life to the effects of extremely delicate sfumato in the represention of the complexion and the wonderful lightness of the hair as it cascades in shimmering ripples. The landscape in the background, which echoes the wide valley in the Uffizi drawing, is similarly wrapped in an atmospheric space that seems, through a mixture of form, colour and light, to blend the various elements of nature in a cosmic synthesis.

Still clearly influenced by the teaching of An-

Study for the Adoration of the Magi *(facsimile),*
c. 1481. Gabinetto dei disegni e delle stampe degli Uffizi,
Florence. (Original in the Cabinet des dessins, Louvre, Paris).

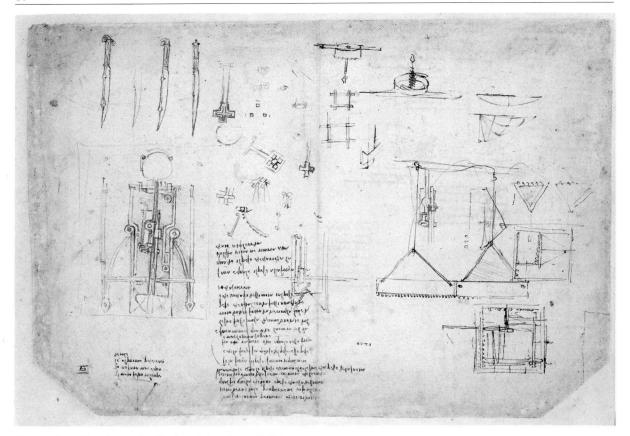

Sheet of studies from the Codex Atlanticus, *f. 27 v.-r. 1483-1518. Biblioteca Ambrosiana, Milan.*

drea Verrocchio, in whose workshop Leonardo remained at least until 1476, is the Uffizi *Annunciation* (Plate 4).

The overall composition of the scene—with the angel on the left separated from the Virgin by a lectern, here imaginatively invented on the basis of an antique model, the horizon placed two-thirds of the way up the picture and the villa behind the Madonna—should be attributed to a compositional pattern which was already in use and reveals the influence of a certain academic rigidity. But the extraordinary sequence of tones and luminosity of the image, the meticulous attention given to the elements of the natural world and the stupendously atmospheric quality with which the landscape beyond the low garden wall is depicted, confer on the painting a distinction and charm which is already very definitely typical of Leonardo's manner.

The subsequent works increasingly emphasized the progressive formation in the artist's mind of a concept of painting as an ideal expres-

sion of his scientific knowledge. The evolution of his style, therefore, was invariably a consequence of the development of his thought.

The portrait of *Ginevra de' Benci* (Plate 6), painted between 1474 and 1477, has proved to be of great interest. The woman, who was portrayed contrary to the aesthetic canons of Botticelli which were dominant at the time—with their expression of extreme linear sensitivity and a timeless ideal of female beauty—and presents strongly individual facial features, artistically created by means of colour and light. In fact, the almost full-face portrayal of the girl allowed the artist to reduce the role of the linear profile to a minimum. The face, with its large flattened volumes, is delicately modelled by extremely subtle gradations of tone, while its pale luminosity is resplendent against the background of a spiky bush which is silhouetted against the sky, allowing us to glimpse, at the sides, a landscape of water and trees.

Shortly after this Leonardo executed two

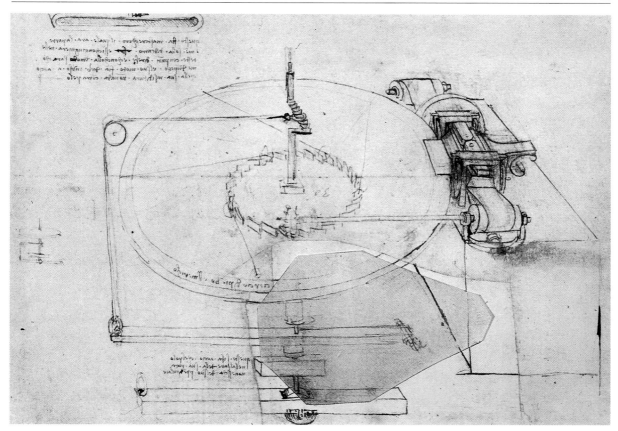

Sheet of studies from the Codex Atlanticus, *f. 31 v.-r.*
1483-1518. Biblioteca Ambrosiana, Milan.

paintings, both depicting the Virgin and Child. The *Virgin with the Flowers* (Plate 7), although there are close analogies with the paintings of Leonardo's earliest period and those which were produced by his master's workshop, displays stylistic features which were then to become typical of the artist. The light which penetrates from the arched windows in the background and, at the same time, illuminates the image from the front, is diffused over the figures making their stately volumes vibrate and giving the flesh the first extremely delicate effect of sfumato. On the other hand, a warmer chromatic density of light and a more accentuated rounding of the forms are characteristic of the *Benois Madonna* (Plate 8), which was probably painted around 1478. The composition of the painting pivots on the small flower which the Virgin is offering to the Infant Christ. Around it revolves the tender interplay of hands and the exchange of glances of the protagonists, who are completely engrossed in the intimacy of this family scene. The complete sty-

listic maturity of the artist is emphasized by the way the bodies of the Madonna and Child fit naturally together (in fact they are placed according to carefully studied schemes of diagonal recession, which are in opposition but are extraordinarily well-balanced), by the sfumato of the soft outlines of the figures, which seem to quiver with life and vibrate in the density of the atmosphere, and, above all, by the great sensitivity with which the intimate emotional bonds linking mother and child are depicted.

However, the painting which bears witness to the great progress which the artist had made in his ceaseless inquiry into the basic principles of nature and the deepest secrets of the human soul before his departure for Milan is the *Adoration of the Magi* (Plate 10). After he had received the commission in 1481, Leonardo interpreted the traditional subject in a revolutionary and intensely dramatic manner, with all his interest focused on the profound religious significance of Christ's birth. The crowd, greatly perturbed by the event, is gathered around the figure of the Virgin and Child, the pivot of the whole composition. The Magi prostrate themselves as they offer their gifts, while the gesticulating crowd is not able to control its feelings and the agitation of its movements seems to be transmitted from one figure to another. In the background the magnificent architectural ruins and the skirmish of warriors on horseback symbolise that part of the world and of humanity not yet aware of the promise of salvation. All the figures, which are strongly individualised in their movements and expressions, are brought alive by means of the usual extremely delicate chiaroscuro effects which soften the outlines and appear to cause the single images to merge with each other and with the surrounding space. Despite its unfinished state, the painting seemed to confirm that the artist's style had reached complete maturity and was an overture to all the works that Leonardo was to produce subsequently.

Not very distant from the unfinished painting of the *Adoration of the Magi* was *Saint Jerome* (Plate 11), which was probably the last work prepared by Leonardo before he left Florence. The particular posture of the figure gives special emphasis to Leonardo's anatomical interests, which were focused at that time on problems concerning the dynamics of the human body in space. The repentant saint, depicted as he beats his breast, is kneeling down or is about to stand up, as is shown by the bending of the knee, while the sculptural representation of the body fits in very well with the extreme fluidity of the painting's execution.

The Milanese Period (1482-1499)

When Leonardo reached Milan some time between the spring and the summer of 1482 he found a particularly lively and stimulating intellectual climate. During the time of Ludovico il Moro the Sforza court became, almost in competition with Florence, a refined centre of the liberal arts, which attracted scientists, artists and men of letters such as Bramante, the mathematician Luca Pacioli and the musician Franchino Gaffurio. The genuine interest of the Sforzas in the most brilliant and culturally up-to-date personalities of the time gave Leonardo the opportunity not only to give free rein to his artistic bent,

but also to develop his studies of nature and science and to display his technical skills in the field of military engineering and architecture, hydraulics and town planning. In fact, by giving prominence to these skills, in the famous draft of the letter addressed to Ludovico il Moro in which he offered his services, Leonardo showed he was perfectly aware of the opportunities which his knowledge could procure for him in that political situation. Firstly he listed all the complex siege engines, the various types of bombards and the curious military systems of attack and defence which he had invented. Lastly, almost as an afterthought, he mentioned his artistic gifts, and he also referred to the enormous equestrian statue of Franceso Sforza, Ludovico's father, which was to be erected to the everlasting glory of the family. Leonardo dedicated himself to this project, on and off, for many years and precious remains of his studies for it are to be found in the numerous preliminary drawings which have come down to us. However, the fall of Sforza rule in 1499 and the consequent departure of the artist from Milan, prevented the casting of the huge bronze monument. For a number of years the enormous clay model of just the horse survived, but it was then destroyed by the French troops of Louis XII.

During his sixteen-year stay in Milan Leonardo's exceptional versatility in various fields of science, technology and art seem to have been in almost constant demand by the Sforza court. In fact, he could be seen hard at work around 1489-1490 as the brilliant inventor of elaborate stage machinery and mechanical contrivances for jousts and court pageants, as a designer of costumes for masquerades and tournaments and as a skilled improviser of poetry, fables and riddles. In the same period, as an expert on architecture, he applied himself to studying the problem of the tambour of Milan cathedral and he was consulted, together with Francesco di Giorgio Martini about the completion of Pavia cathedral. In his role as court engineer he tackled the question of schemes involving the management of water in the area, planning locks, canals and irrigation systems. In particular, around 1494, he was concerned with irrigation and drainage works at La Sforzesca, the ducal estate near Vigevano.

But it was above all as a painter that Leonardo, by further developing the research he had started in Florence, revealed a capacity that was so innovative that it upset the traditional canons of Lombard painting of the time, which could, however, boast such remarkable painters as Vincenzo Foppa, Ambrogio Bergognone and Bernardo Zenale. The paintings of the Milanese period display a perfect balance between linearity and perspective, an achievement of the Florentine Renaissance, and use of light and atmosphere, typical of the Lombard school in the second half of the Quattrocento. At the same time, however, they also display a deliberate reworking of both stylistic languages in a manner that was totally original and revolutionary. The first example in Milan of this new artistic vision was the painting known as the *Virgin of the Rocks*, central altarpiece of the polyptych executed from 1483 onwards for the altar of a chapel in the church of San Francesco Grande. It was commissioned by the Confraternity of the Immaculate Conception and was painted with the collaboration of the brothers Evangelista and Ambrogio de' Predis (Plates 12, 13; Plates 14-16).

First of all, the painting expresses a new vision of nature, which is no longer merely reproduced, but is created anew by the artist by means of a careful analysis of its phenomena. Consequently there is a new way of depicting space, which is no longer conceived according to the principles of perspective, but rather it is created "naturally" by means of the atmosphere, that is to say by the almost imperceptible fusion of air, light and shade that at the same time both envelopes and forms everything. The figures, too, rather than being created through the traditional use of drawing and chiaroscuro, are produced by the natural effect of light and imperceptible gradations of shade on their bodies, which thus acquire the extreme delicacy of their lineaments and the subtle plasticity which are the very basis of Leonardo's sfumato.

The immediate repercussion of this new way of looking at art on the painters of the Lombard school could be noticed — with an effect that was perhaps even more disruptive — in portraiture, a field in which Leonardo introduced a real artistic revolution to Milan. In fact, the *Portrait of a Musician* in the Pinacoteca Ambrosiana (Plate 17), the *Lady with an Ermine* in Cracow (Plates 18,

Study for the head of Saint James the Apostle in the Last Supper and architectural studies, *c. 1495. Royal Library, Windsor Castle.*

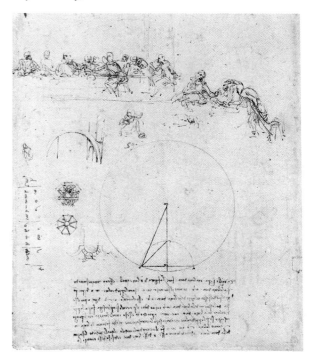

Study for the Last Supper and architectural studies, *c. 1495. Royal Library, Windsor Castle.*

19) and the portrait of a lady in the Louvre, known as *La Belle Ferronnière* (Plates 20, 21), threw the traditional concepts of Milanese portraitists into disarray, accustomed as they were to portraying the sitter with a profile view, in accordance with a taste which was still typically heraldic.

While the attribution of the *Portrait of a Musician* in the Pinacoteca Ambrosiana has often been debated in the past, more recent scholarly opinion has generally agreed that it is by the hand of Leonardo, in some cases, however, accepting that there may have been limited assistance by Ambrogio de' Predis in the lower part of the painting. The portrait makes it very clear which direction Leonardo's pictorial research was taking him. The sitter's bust, which seems to revolve in space and intersect the surface of the painting obliquely, and the keen psychological insight of the face, with its firmly incisive modelling, which does not, however, overlook the most minute detail, are all expressions of his increasingly profound studies of the dynamics of the body and the representation of the workings of the human soul.

The same elements are arranged with greater compositional skill and a better command of painting techniques in the *Lady with an Ermine*, which may be considered to be one of the highest expressions of Leonardo's art, fruit of the anatomical studies to which the artist had devoted himself for many years, as is clearly shown by the drawings which can be admired on the pages of his notebooks. The bust of the girl, a masterpiece of grace and elegance, forms a sinuous spiral in space and concludes splendidly with a face which displays an extraordinary expression of intensity and restrained emotion. The image is infused with life, in a way that recalls painting from northern Europe or the work of Antonello da Messina, by the shaft of light that practically shapes its structure, illuminating the lady's face, descending her shoulder and falling on her arms which hug the brilliantly white ermine.

The climax of Leonardo's activity in Milan, and one of the great masterpieces of the Renaissance, is the *Last Supper*, which was painted between 1495 and 1497 in the refectory of the monastery of Santa Maria delle Grazie (Plates 22-24). In fact, it is the conclusion, at their highest point,

of his carefully meditated studies of the human spirit. On hearing Christ firmly announce His imminent betrayal, the Apostles' great excitement seems to abate, and then take artistic form in harmonious unity, through the skilled arrangement of the forms, movements and gestures of the figures, depicted larger-than-life and rhythmically grouped in threes. Also the way the perspective is constructed—thereby extending and amplifying through the use of illusionistic effects the real architectural space of the room—and the brightly-lit landscape that it is possible to see through the windows in the background lend the whole scene unprecedented strength and monumental grandeur.

In the last years of his presence at the Milanese court Leonardo worked, in his capacity as ducal engineer, at the Sforza Castle. The decoration of the Sala delle Asse, which was executed with a considerable amount of assistance, is invaluable evidence of this activity, even though, unfortunately, it has been largely lost or repainted. From the base of the walls rises a regular sequence of enormous tree trunks which penetrate the rocky terrain with their roots and, interrupted by patches of sky, reach upwards with thickly intertwining branches, according to an extremely complex composition which is, however, arranged in a thoroughly logical manner. A forest of branches, foliage and fruit, expressing the immense force of nature, covers the ceiling of the room, which the artist transformed into a leafy cupola. In the centre, surrounded by a system of cords and branches dotted with small red berries, appears the coat of arms of the Sforza family, which forms the pivot of the whole composition and is symbol of the strength of wise government that imposes order and stability on the complexities of the world. Through the use of illusionism the closed area of the room was thus expanded and transformed into an open space, the concrete fulfilment of Leonardo's concept of nature interpreted as an expression of life and of painting seen as a powerful means of creation.

The Mature Years (1500-1519)

Following the sudden fall of the Sforzas with the invasion of the French troops of Louis XII, Leonardo, who was now famous all over Italy, left

Milan together with his friend, Luca Pacioli. It is very likely that he took with him manuscripts covered with notes and observations, together with loose sheets, notebooks and sketchpads crammed with profiles, portraits, caricatures, faces of monstrous or deformed beings and anatomical details which were astonishing for the beauty and precision of the draughtsmanship. These were all precious evidence of the studies of the human figure which he carried out during his stay in Milan.

After a brief stay in Vaprio d'Adda, at the home of his favourite pupil, Francesco Melzi, Leonardo went to Mantua, where he was a guest of the Gonzagas for a brief period. In an attempt to prevent him from leaving, Isabella d'Este commissioned her portrait, the cartoon for which, executed in black chalk and pastels, is now in the Louvre.

In March 1500 Leonardo stayed in Venice in order to offer his services as a military engineer, then in August of that year, after an eighteen-year absence, he returned to Florence, where he was a guest in the monastery of the Serviti alla Santissima Annunziata. He stayed there, apart from brief interruptions, until 1506. In this period—despite the fact that contemporary sources described him as being increasingly fascinated by the study of science and immersed in mathematical experiments—the artist executed paintings which constituted the basis for the evolution of the entire art of the Cinquecento.

A composition with Saint Anne, the Virgin and Child and the infant Saint John seemed to capture Leonardo's attention at that time. In fact, this is simply a further development of a theme—that of the pyramidal structure—which had been tackled previously in the *Virgin of the Rocks*. The importance which this theme had acquired in his creative activity is evidenced by the cartoon in the National Gallery in London (Plate 27) and the painting in the Louvre (Plates 29, 30), which probably date from the beginning of the second decade of the sixteenth century, as well as a large number of sketches and preliminary drawings.

The London cartoon displays a wonderful balance between art and nature and between matter and spirit. The masterly construction of the group and the compactness and the monu-

mental grandeur of the forms match the naturalness of the movements of the figures, the delicate flow of the drapery, the expressive intensity of the faces and the infinite gentleness of the glances. Mary, Saint Anne, the Child and the infant Saint John are the complete expression of the poetry of the "spirit and breath" which was so characteristic of the Apostles in the *Last Supper*, but with a more restrained and profound emotional content, and displaying faultlessness of form which became a manifestation of the harmonious perfection of creation. The painting, now in the Louvre, constitutes the conclusive point of the research. The solidity and compactness of the London group is broken up in the Paris painting by more accentuated dynamics of the forms. The "vibrations" which seem to emanate from the rocks in the foreground and the masterly organisation of the movements of the figures—they spontaneously intertwine, embrace each other and then separate in accordance with a harmonious flow of rhythms that have been carefully calculated but seem to be natural—are then subjected by the artist to rational vision. The variety of the phenomena of reality is thus expressed through a geometrical composition which reflects the absolute harmony of the universe, nature and art.

In 1502 Leonardo spent a brief period as architect and military engineer in the employ of Cesare Borgia, the ambitious son of Pope Alexander VI who, with the support of his father, had managed to form his own state in Romagna and central Italy.

On his return to Florence in March 1503, the artist was commissioned by the gonfalonier (chief magistrate) of the Republic, Pier Soderini, to paint an enormous fresco celebrating the victory of the Florentines over the Milanese troops of Filippo Maria Visconti in the famous battle of Anghiari in 1440 on one of the walls of the new Sala del Gran Consiglio in Palazzo Vecchio. The available documentary evidence gives a very detailed description of the artistic creation, so that it is possible to follow the various stages, almost as if we were present in person. These stages range from the preliminary sketches to the splendid drawing of the cartoon (Plates 31, 32), from the construction of the scaffolding in the room to the purchase of the materials—gesso, linseed oil, colophony and white lead—which were needed to prepare the wall, from the disastrous results of the first layer of plaster to the transposition to the wall of the central part of the magnificent composition, right up to the moment when painting itself started.

In the same period the Florentine Republic commissioned the young Michelangelo, the celebrated sculptor of *David*, to paint, in the same room, frescos of the analogous theme of the battle of Cascina. Unfortunately Michelangelo did not get any further than the cartoon, which was destroyed in 1512 when the Medicis came back to power in Florence, while Leonardo's fragmentary painting disappeared as a result of the rebuilding of the room and the painting of new pictures by Vasari in 1557. The cartoons of the two geniuses of the Italian Renaissance were the "school of the world"—as Benvenuto Cellini put it—for generations of artists to come. Neither drawings of the whole painting nor details of the subsidiary motives of Leonardo's majestic work have survived. It is only through a number of engravings and a few copies—the most famous is the drawing by Rubens now in the Louvre—that the central motive of the composition is known to us. This was the furious struggle of horses and horsemen for the conquest of the standard, the symbol of the city.

In 1506 Leonardo once again left Florence for Milan, where he had been invited by the French governor, Charles d'Amboise. Besides the *Battle of Anghiari* (Plates 31, 32), while he was in Florence he had begun—according to Vasari—the portrait of *Mona Lisa* (Plates 35, 36) and the painting, which was later lost, of *Leda with the Swan* (Plate 26). These were evidence, together with a number of drawings depicting *Neptune with the Seahorses*, of the artist's interest in mythological themes, in particular those which could become the embodiment of the power of nature, both of the generative and vehement varieties.

In Milan he stayed, with occasional brief interruptions, until 1513. Here he engaged in architectural and hydraulic engineering work, he devoted himself to the study of the equestrian statue for Gian Giacomo Trivulzio (1511-1512), executed the painting of the *Virgin and Saint Anne* (Plates 29, 30) now in the Louvre and, lastly, with assistants, completed the second version

of the *Virgin of the Rocks* (Plates 14-16). In this period Leonardo was increasingly absorbed by mathematical and scientific studies; he investigated these interests more thoroughly in Rome, where he moved in 1513. In this city he was accommodated in the Vatican in the Villa del Belvedere with the patronage of Giuliano de' Medici. The artist, who by this time was getting on in years, was averse to the ostentation of the Roman art milieu, which was dominated by Raphael and his circle. Generally leading an isolated life, he executed, among other things, an extraordinary series of drawings on the theme of the *Deluge* (Plate 37), which clearly reveal the unease of the later years of the great artist's life and the crisis of his notion of man as the centre of the universe and mirror of its harmonious perfection. Besides this, during the years he was in Milan and Rome, Leonardo returned to the theme of the human figure, completing two works of maximum interest—the so-called *Bacchus* (Plate 33) and *Saint John the Baptist* (Plate 34)—which embody a new ideal of beauty which was ambiguous and indeterminate and which was wholly realized in the *Mona Lisa* (Plates 35, 36). This painting, together with *Saint John the Baptist* and the *Virgin and Saint Anne*, was taken by the artist to France in 1517. Loaded with honours, designated by Francis I "premier peintre architecte et méchanicien du roi," Leonardo resided in the château of Cloux, near Amboise, until his death on 2 May 1519, dedicating himself to his research and to his perturbing drawings on the theme of the *Deluge*.

Leonardo spent a great deal of time on the portrait of a lady, which he began sometime between 1503 and 1506 and which was to become the most famous of all his paintings, working on it until his final years, in a ceaseless quest for formal perfection. The painting, therefore, embodied all Leonardo's experience and was the sublime synthesis of his studies of natural phenomena and of the movements of the human body that the artist had tackled, investigated in depth and attempted to give tangible form to for all his life. The woman in the portrait, who has recently been interpreted—in close harmony with the landscape in the background—as the symbol of the triumph of Chastity over Time, does not, therefore, embody an ideal of female beauty, but, although she has a strongly individualised personality, she becomes the crystallisation of the human individual who sums up in herself, with perfect balance, all the possible states of nature.

It is through the medium of painting, taken to a level of extreme technical refinement, that we are able to comprehend the profundity of Leonardo's thought. The passages of tone, colour and luminosity, which are ever subtler and more delicate, the sfumato which is ever softer and more enveloping and layers of glazes which are ever lighter and more transparent, confer on the forms of the woman's body, as well as on the mountains and the expanses of water in the landscape, that margin of indeterminacy which is the expression of perpetual transformation and the eternal renewal of life and nature. Artistic creation, and especially painting, which Leonardo considered to be the most noble of the arts, in the *Mona Lisa* is, therefore, a concrete expression of nature, a means of investigating the reality of the world and of human thought.

The Legacy

Leonardo da Vinci's legacy is enormous. The exceptional nature of his talent, the multiplicity of his practical skills and the power of his intellect were already universally recognised during his lifetime, while his fame and prestige have never ceased to grow over the centuries. However, it is only relatively recently—more or less from the beginning of the century—that besides Leonardo the artist, at first timorously and then, in time, more clearly, thanks to continuous scholarly inquiry, an unknown Leonardo has begun to take shape. The unfamiliar figure who has been rediscovered, but about whom there is still a lot to learn, made important contributions to mathematics, optics, physics and science in general. The influence of his painting on the art of the Cinquecento, especially bearing in mind the very

limited number of works which can be attributed to him with certainty, is inestimable. Paintings such as the *Virgin of the Rocks* or the *Last Supper*, portraits like the *Musician* and the *Lady with an Ermine* were a constant point of reference for the later generations of Lombard painters, who immediately assimilated Leonardo's iconographic and stylistic innovations, albeit with results that were sometimes decidedly mediocre. Obviously the effects of Leonardo's art were not limited just to Lombardy, but had far-reaching repercussions all over Europe in the sixteenth century. Thus Giorgione, Dürer, Raphael, Michelangelo and Correggio could not help but continuously refer to Leonardo's masterpieces and compare their own work with his.

Leonardo has always enjoyed undisputed critical and literary acclaim. But the mythical nineteenth century image of the great—but admittedly somewhat eccentric—artistic genius for a long time prevented a more objective study of his personality. Only in the last few decades has the study, transcription and interpretation of the great quantity of drawings and annotations entrusted to the surviving codices thrown new light on the romantic picture of the artist. In its place there is another, still greater image of Leonardo, which is slowly taking shape on a historical and philological basis. Besides this, various important research projects have continued to widen our knowledge of the artist's output of paintings. The analysis of his sketches and preparatory drawings, the study of surviving copies and erroneous or disputed attributions and the use of sophisticated technical instruments to investigate the paintings allow us to piece together a more accurate picture of Leonardo's legacy. Although it is still largely unexplored, this legacy is a necessary starting point for a full understanding of the life and personality of the "greatest artistic project of the Renaissance" (L.M. Batkin, 1988).

Anthology

A given volume of air is full of innumerable pyramids of light, which are produced by the bodies placed in them. These pyramids, which intersect and intertwine, without invading each other, spread out into the surrounding air, and they all have equal power: they all have the same power as each one and each one has the power of all of them... All bodies have impressed on the air and mixed with it all their characteristics or likenesses to the same extent as the air which is opposed to these bodies. The characteristics of each point of the surfaces of a body are to be found in every point of this air. The characteristics of these bodies are to be found each point of the air. The characteristics of the air are to be found in their totality in every part of the surface of the bodies opposed to them. Hence all of the characteristics of the bodies appear wholly and in part opposed to the air and the volume of air appears to be wholly or partly opposed to the surface of these bodies. Thus we can say clearly that the characteristic of each body is to be found interchangeably in each part and in the whole of the opposed bodies.
(Leonardo da Vinci, *Codex Atlanticus*, f. 101 v., 1483-1518, Biblioteca Ambrosiana, Milan)

A definition of the existence of the line: the line itself does not have any matter or substance, but it can more easily be called a *thing of spirit* rather than a thing of substance, and because it is conditioned by this it does not occupy any space. Hence it is possible to imagine that innumerable lines intersect at one point, which is not divisible and the thickness of which (if, indeed, it is possible to speak of thickness) is equal to the thickness of just one line.
(Leonardo da Vinci, *Manuscripts and Drawings*, 1489-1516, Royal Library, Windsor Castle)

The moon does not have its own light, except when the sun illuminates it. We see this lunar light in the same way that an observer on the moon would see the luminosity of the earth. And the lunar night receives as much light as do the waters which are on the terrestrial surface when they reflect the image of the sun, and the moon is reflected in those terrestrial waters which reflect the sun. The surface of the water which forms the lunar sea and the sea of our earth is always to a greater or lesser extent covered with waves; and this waviness is the cause of the spreading of a great number of images of the sun which are reflected in the ridges and hollows and sides and fronts of the innumerable waves, that is to say in many different places of each wave, so many are the places which can be seen by our eyes. Now this could not happen if the sphere of water which covers a large part of the moon was uniformly spherical, because then there would be one image of the sun in each eye, and its reflection would be singular and it would always be spherical brightness, as the gilded balls on the tops of high buildings clearly indicate. But if these gilded balls were corrugated and covered with small globes, as is the blackberry, a black fruit composed of small round sections, then each part of these globularities seen by the sun and the eye will show this eye the brilliance produced by the image of the sun. And so in the same body would be seen a large number of very small suns, which very often, due to the fact that they are seen from a great distance, would join together and seem to be one.

(Leonardo da Vinci, *Codex Arundel* 263, f. 94 r., 1504-1516, British Museum, London)

The painter, or rather draughtsman, has to be solitary, above all when he is busy with speculations and reflections, which, as they continuously appear before his eyes, provide arguments for the memory which should be carefully retained... The eye, in which the splendour of the universe is reflected by the observer, is so excellent that anyone who permits it to be lost, deprives himself of the sight of all the works of nature, in order to see which the soul is content to abide in the prison of the human body, through whose eyes the soul perceives all the various wonders of Nature.

(Leonardo da Vinci, *Trattato della Pittura, Codex Vaticano Latino 1270*, c. 1550, Biblioteca Vaticana, Rome)

If the painter wishes to see things of beauty that will enchant him, he may create them. If he wants to see monstrous things that frighten people, or that are clownish and ridiculous, or are truly pitiful then he is free to do it. And if he wishes to create places and wildernesses and cool shady nooks in hot weather, he will paint them, and so will he depict hot places in cold weather. If he desires valleys, if he wishes to cast his eyes over great expanses of countryside from high mountain peaks and if he then wants to observe the horizon of the sea, it is within his power to do so. And the same is true if from low valleys he wishes to see high mountains or from the high mountains he wishes to see low valleys and beaches. And, in effect, that which is in the universe because it is of the essence or because it is present or is an invention, he has first of all in his mind and then in his hands. And these are so excellent that with the same speed they create proportioned harmony at a single glance, just as the natural world does.

(Leonardo da Vinci, *Trattato della pittura, Codex Vaticano Latino 1270*, c. 1550, Biblioteca Vaticana, Rome)

There were in Milan at the time of Viscount Ludovico Sforza, Duke of Milan, some gentlemen in the monastery of the Grazie of the monks of the Dominican order, and in the refectory they stood in silence observing the miraculous and famous last supper of Christ with his disciples which the excellent Florentine painter Leonardo da Vinci was painting at that time, and he was very anxious that whosoever saw his work should freely express his opinion regarding it. He would go there early in the morning and climb up on the scaffolding, because the painting is quite high above the ground. On numerous occasions, and I have seen this with my own eyes, he would not put his brush down from sunrise to dusk, but, forgetting to eat and drink, he would continue to paint. There were then two, three or even four days in which he did not touch his painting, yet he stood sometimes one or two hours a day just looking at it and then he examined it carefully and passed judgements on the figures. I also saw him, when the whim took him, leave at midday, with the sun in the sign of Leo, from the Corte Vecchia where he was making that stupendous clay horse, and come straight to the Grazie, climb onto the scaffolding, take up his brush, give one or two touches to one of the figures and then straightaway leave for another place.

(Matteo Bandello, Novella LVIII, in *Novelle*, 1497)

Great gifts are seen to rain down from the celestial spheres on human beings. Often naturally, and sometimes supernaturally, in a single being are excessively concentrated beauty, grace and virtue in such a manner that—whatever this individual may turn his hand to—every action of his is so divine that, leaving all other men behind him, it is manifestly recognised as a thing which only God can bestow and is not acquired by human art. Men saw this quality in Leonardo da Vinci, who, apart from the beauty of his body, which was never lauded sufficiently, displayed infinite grace in everything that he did; and so great was his virtue and such was its nature that, whatever difficult thing he turned his attention to, he was able to conclude with the greatest of ease... Because nature desired to favour him, wherever he turned his thought, mind or spirit, he displayed such excellence in his actions that his perfection of eagerness, vivacity, goodness, handsomeness and charm were never equalled by anyone else. It should be noted that, because of his great ability in art, Leonardo began many things, but did not complete any of them, as it appeared to him that his hand could not add anything to the perfection of art in the things he invented. Moreover he formed in his mind such subtle and wondrous problems that with his hands, however excellent they might have been, he could not have ever created them. And so many were his fantasies that, when philosophising about natural things, he would dedicate himself to studying the properties of grasses and then would go on to observe the motion of the heavens, the phases of the moon and the path of the sun... It is a wonderful thing that this great master, who, wishing to give maximum relief to the things that he was painting, made such great use of dark shades that he produced dark backgrounds that required blacks that might create gradations of colour and were darker than the other blacks, with the result that the light colours were so much brighter.

Finally he was able to produce a style which was so dark that, as nothing light remained, it seemed to depict a night scene rather than something seen by light of day. But all this was an attempt to give greater relief, to find the true purpose of art and attain perfection... In the art of painting he added to the manner of using oil paints a certain darkness, by means of which modern painters have derived strength and relief for their figures.

(G. Vasari, *Delle Vite de' più eccellenti pittori, scultori et architettori*, 1568, 1906 edition)

Leonardo's character is to be found in his nobility of spirit, in the lucidity of his inventiveness, the breadth of his knowledge, thought and deeds and his wise counsel, which were united to his handsome appearance, justice, reason, wisdom and the separation of right from wrong, the sublimity of light from the baseness of obscurity and ignorance from the boundless glory of truth and charity, the queen of all virtues... In his painting he was dependent on the greatness of his drawing and he achieved this so completely that the figures of men, whether of noble station or humble, were depicted with a great spate of painting, meticulously portraying their characteristics, giving them light and shade as necessary by means of many layers of paint. And in the smaller details, such as the caps, flowing locks and hair in general, flowers, grass, stones and especially the drapery, he so wonderfully and with such skill applied the paint that no mortal eye could desire anything further... When painting light Leonardo showed that he always wanted to avoid making it too bright, to create a better effect, and he tried to make the dark colours very intense so as to discover their utmost limits. Therefore, with this art he achieved in the faces and the bodies, which he painted marvellously, everything that nature can create. And in this role he was superior to everyone else, to the extent that, in a word, we can describe Leonardo's genius as being divine.

(G.P. Lomazzo, *Idea del Tempio della pittura*, 1590)

Leonardo da Vinci was born before Michelangelo Buonarroti, and he was endowed with a less resolute genius, which was less extensive but more noble... He had two manners of painting: one made use of dark colours which allowed the light colours to stand out marvellously; ... the other was a calmer style and was effected by means of half-tones ... In all his styles the grace of his drawing, the expression of his nature and the subtlety of his brushwork triumphed.

(L. Lanzi, *Storia pittorica della Italia*, 1792)

Even though he was a universal genius, Leonardo revealed his greatness above all in his painting. As he was proportioned regularly and perfectly, in comparison with common men he appeared to be an ideal example of humanity. Just as the lucidity and the keenness of the sight refer more appropriately to the intellect, so lucidity and intelligence were peculiar to the artist. He never yielded to the sudden impulses of his matchless original talent and, curbing every spontaneous and fortuitous instinct, he desired that every detail should be pondered over at length. From his research into pure proportions to his figures of the most hybrid monsters, everything had to appear natural and rational.
(Johann Wolfgang Goethe, *Italian Journey*, 1816)

The *Mona Lisa* is Leonardo's masterpiece in the true sense of the word. It is the example which reveals his way of thinking and working. As far as fascination is concerned, only Dürer's *Melancholia* can be compared with this work, but with the difference that no confused symbolism disturbs the effect of his painting, which is mysterious, profound and very graceful ... She is more ancient than the rocks among which she is seated. Like a vampire, she died many times and discovered the secrets of the grave. She inhabited deep seas and absorbed their fading light. She traded in strange fabrics with the merchants of the East and, like Leda, was mother of Helen of Troy and, like Saint Anne, was mother of Mary. And for her everything was no more than the music of flutes and lyres, and she only came alive in the delicacy with which the changeable lineaments assumed an expression and the eyelids and hands gained colour. The concept of an eternal life which collects thousands of experiences dates back to ancient times, and modern philosophy has conceived the idea of humanity as a product of this and as the sum total of all the ways of life and systems of thought. Certainly, therefore, Mona Lisa could be considered to be an expression of the imagination of the ancient world and a symbol of modernity.
(W. Pater, *Studies in the History of the Renaissance*, 1873)

Of a man remains only what attracts us in his name and the works which made that name into a symbol of admiration, hate and indifference. As if it were the doing of a mechanism, a hypothesis manifests itself, and there appears the individual who has done everything, the central vision in which everything must have happened, the prodigious mind or strange animal which has woven thousands of pure bonds between many forms, and of which those many enigmatic constructions were the anguish, the instinct which stayed behind. I intend to imagine a man of whom such remarkable actions have appeared that if I decide to suppose that in them there is a thought, there could not be a more extensive one. And I would like him to have an awareness of the difference between things which is infinitely profound, and whose destiny could well be called analysis. I would like everything to orientate him; he is always thinking of the universe and of rigour. His character does not allow him to forget anything which takes part in the confusion of existence—not even a shrub. He lowers himself into the profundity which is common to all, he goes away from it and contemplates himself; he draws on natural habits and structures, he works on them in all their parts, and he finds that he is the only one who builds, enumerates and instigates. He leaves churches and fortresses standing, creates ornaments which are full of sweetness and grandeur, a thousand tools and the precise drawings of some research project and he abandons the remnants of who knows what great games. In these pastimes, into which is introduced his science, which is no different from a passion, he takes a delight in always seeming to be thinking of something else... It will follow him while he moves in the crude unity and reality of the world, in which he will become so intimate with nature that he will imitate it in order to reach it, and will end up by finding it difficult to conceive of an object which is not contained in it. There lacks a name for this creature of intellect, so as to understand the extent of terms which are normally too far apart and would be lost. None seems to me more fitting than that of Leonardo da Vinci... The majority of people see with their minds much more often than with their eyes. Instead of areas of colour they become aware of concepts... The use of the opposite gift leads to authentic analysis... For this reason it is necessary to place the observer who can see well in any corner of existence. The observer is closed in a sphere which never breaks, in which there are differences that will be movements and objects and whose surface remains whole, even though all its parts are renewed and move inside it. I can see Leonardo da Vinci investigating more closely that mechanism which he called the paradise of the sciences with the same natural vigour with which he devoted himself to the invention of pure faces with softened outlines. And the same shining expanse, with its feasible docile beings, is the place in which actions calmly form themselves into separate works. On the last page of his thin notebook—consumed by his secret writing and daring calculations in which he grapples with the problems of his favourite research project, aviation—he shouts, railing against his imperfect work and illuminating his patience and the obstacles with the apparition of a supreme spiritual idea of obstinate certainty: "The great bird on the back of his enormous swan will take to flight for the first time, filling the universe with wonder, and filling all the writings with his fame, to the eternal glory of the nest where he was born." (Paul Valéry, *Introduction à la Méthode de Léonard de Vincy*, 1894)

All that Giotto and Masaccio had attained in the rendering of tactile values, all that Fra Angelico or Filippo had achieved in expression, all that Pollaiuolo had accomplished in movement, or Verrocchio in light and shade, Leonardo, without the faintest trace of that tentativeness, that painfulness of effort which characterized his immediate precursors, equalled or surpassed... And if Leonardo has been left behind as a painter of light, no one has succeeded in conveying by means of light and shade a more penetrating feeling of mystery and awe than he in his *Virgin of the Rocks*. Add to all this a feeling for beauty and significance that have scarcely ever been approached... Leonardo is the one artist of whom it may be said with perfect literalness: Nothing that he touched but turned into a thing of eternal beauty. Whether it be the cross-section of a skull, the structure of a weed, of a study of muscles, he, with his feeling for line and for light and shade, for ever transmuted it into life-communicating values; and all without intention, for most

of these magical sketches were dashed off to illustrate purely scientific matter, which alone absorbed his mind at the moment.
(B. Berenson, *The Italian Painters of the Renaissance*, London 1896)

Nor was Leonardo immune from the human weakness of despising what one does not know and does not possess. On numerous occasions his determined position as rigorous naturalist showed signs of becoming narrow-minded in a way which was typical of those who do not see any other activity as being worthwhile apart from their own. From this derived his advice not to meddle in "those things which the human mind is not capable of and which it is not possible to demonstrate by means of natural example." That which could not be given a mathematical basis, for him, was non-existent ... What we must look for in Leonardo is certainly not a system, which is lacking, but the meaning and importance of a number of observations occurring in his writing that concern aspects of truth which are then explained and justified by the subsequent development of his line of thinking. Thus it is quite remarkable that Leonardo should have generally tended to consider art, especially painting, as a theoretical matter, or a form of knowledge, or "science" as he put it. "If you despise painting, which is the only imitator of all the manifest works of nature, it is certain that you will equally despise a subtle invention, which with philosophical and fine speculation considers all the classes of forms: seas, places, plants, animals, grasses and flowers, which are surrounded by light and shade. And truly this is science, and the legitimate child of nature, because painting is brought forth by nature." Painting never appeared to him merely as an instrument of pleasure, or a means of obtaining practical ends. His mathematical ideal of science, in the presence of his knowledge of painting, caused him some embarrassment. However, he recognised that painting offered something more than, or different from, what mathematics could offer. Geometry and arithmetic "do not expatiate on anything except information regarding continuous or discontinuous quantities, but they are not concerned with quality, which is the beauty of the works of nature and the ornament

of the world." His passion for experience and for the concrete caused him to insist on the value of certainty that art possesses, in that it is sure of the certainty which is so characteristic of the senses. "Painting deals with the appearances, colours and forms of anything created by nature. And philosophy penetrates the same bodies, observing in them its own virtue, but it is not satisfied by the truth produced by the painter, who keeps to himself the fundamental truth of such bodies, so that the eye might be less beguiled."
(B. Croce, "Leonardo filosofo," in *Leonardo*, 1939)

It is necessary to ask what the meaning of the onset of the particular problem of "light and shade" was. It is useless to suppose that it contains even a hint of problems of tone or colour, or even of an impressionistic nature. Leonardo's anti-impressionistic project was fairly definite when he urged that leaves which are transparent in the sun should never be simulated because they are indistinct. How could it have been otherwise for an artist who believed that painting's moment of greatest dignity was "showing relief on a plane?"
If necessary there was the preferred tradition of abstract chiaroscuro in "universal light," and Leonardo was certainly not prepared to do without this. Thus he decided to cloud it over, to tone it down, to soften it. This was an accommodation that, on that basis, could not have found its own procedure, but could only have pointed allusively to a desire for sentimental and poetic escapism in a twilit evening world, in the "dark air," that "certain obscurity" which Vasari mentioned. And he stayed like that, in conflict with his original genius for vital lucidity and even with his rituals of classical equilibrium. It was then that his thoughts and figures appeared mistily with their soft outlines from caves in the Lombard foothills of the Alps, which Leonardo the speleologist had already explored. It was not, therefore, at all strange that this latter excogitation, more than all the rest, should have pleased the romantics and decadents of the last century, who were much more interested in mysteries than in clear explanations.
(R. Longhi, "Difficoltà di Leonardo," in *Paragone*, 29, 1952)

The final conclusions of Leonardo the scientist took shape in artistic creations. In these the magnificent unitary nature of his scientific and artistic concepts and the indivisible bonds between them were displayed once again... The extent to which he was fully conscious of all this is indicated by his own words: "Nature is full of infinite reasons which have never been part of experience." Until the very last moment of his life Leonardo was obsessed by the idea that there should exist supernatural universal harmony which functioned in all forms, forces and spatial and temporal dimensions and which would manifest itself as such even in the apparent chaos of the end of the world. He attempted to find this harmony in all the phenomena which his inquiring mind might observe and he did his best to depict them in every artistic creation of his. Art was, then, both an instrument of his research and of his science.
(L.H. Heydenreich, "Leonardo da Vinci," in *Enciclopedia universale dell'arte*, VIII, 1958)

His aesthetic doctrine was unknown until the publication of the manuscripts. Only in 1651 was the *Treatise on Painting* printed, and this was based on a transcript of the sixteenth century. Leonardo's wide-ranging studies had led him to a complete cosmological concept which united heaven and earth in the pulsations of a universe brought alive by radiated light and driven by the constant struggle of the elements. In particular these included water, the basis of the blue atmosphere in which the backgrounds of his paintings were steeped. The crowning glory of all doctrinal wisdom was for him painting, which was the only medium which allowed the beauty and richness of form to be completely extolled.
(A. Chastel, *Storia dell'arte italiana*, 1982)

However, it was Milan that gave birth to Leonardo the theoretician and man of science. His scientific vocation had its origins in his encounter with men of letters, a category which included philosophers, theologians, physicians and, in general, students of the so-called liberal arts. In contrast with them Leonardo represented the world of the "manual" or "menial" arts. It was a social hierarchy which dated back to ancient times, when free men avoided manual work in

order to dedicate themselves to purely intellectual activities, in other words the humanities and philosophy with all the sciences and politics. Physical work in contact with the impure matter was reserved for slaves, freedmen and illiterates, rising up the social scale to artisans and artists, who were still considered, however, to be part of the category of the "manual arts." Leonardo could not abide the underestimation of his art. Painting had to be included with the liberal arts, in so far as it was a science due to its rich store of theory and because it did not confine itself to depicting the surfaces of objects, but it penetrated them and revealed their internal properties and the pulsation of vital energies.
(A. Marinoni, "Il Codice Atlantico," in *Leonardo all'Ambrosiana, il Codice Atlantico, i disegni di Leonardo e della sua cerchia*, edited by A. Marinoni and L. Cogliati Arano, 1982)

The very high opinion which Leonardo had of painting and, consequently, the leading role among all the other artists which he assigned to the painter, led him to speak about an analogy with divine power. But this did not happen because of the typically Renaissance exaltation of the human being as the key figure of the world, but rather through the consciousness of unequalled independent power given to the artist who stands before Nature... As a painter, Leonardo made every effort to attain his own personal style, which was the one that allowed him to surpass the ideals of drawing and plasticity of the Florentine tradition in order to obtain a fully pictorial effect. In this style he attained the fervour of life as it was happening, almost mysteriously, with the imperceptible vibration of shadow, light and tone. It was also the ideal which he had developed by the observation of the world which surrounded him, preferring to be out at twilight in order to enjoy greater intimacy with nature and a subtler, more penetrating exploration of the secrets of life.
(V. Mariani, "Le idee di Leonardo sulla pittura," in *Leonardo da Vinci*, 1984)

Leonardo was right. It was not possible to liken him to contemporary architects, forgers of cannon and so on. This was not because he so brilliantly outshone them all, but because he was concerned with totally different questions. They made weapons of war and built fortresses. He, on the other hand, produced ideas, which were not mere conjectures, but the outcome of the interaction of brain, eye and hand. That is to say he forged himself. His temerity was too magnificent for it to be written off as mere arrogance. It was something else, at least from a historical point of view. It was, in fact, thanks to the chaotic and unfinished state of his projects that in many cases Leonardo's work obtained, with extraordinary completeness, an original result that had not been entirely foreseen. In the immense contradictory alternation of these projects—which was not referable to any common denominator existing among Leonardo's inventions and initiatives—and in their variety, the Inventor was devised, the Conceiver was planned and the singular model of cultural creativity as an end in itself was developed. This gives particular interest to the figure of Leonardo in this century, when, for the first time, culture has become so problematic regarding itself... Michelangelo was the greatest artist of the Renaissance because he was quite simply obliged to be nothing but an artist. Precisely for this reason, his task lay outside the field of art. It was no mere coincidence that Michelangelo's creations became increasingly "non-aesthetic," astonishingly intense, unbearable and non-classical—to put it another way non-Renaissance. For Michelangelo art was obtained by dint of hard physical work, with the carving of stone, with the enervating introjection in the matter, in order to create it again from within... Leonardo developed this idea of a universal "science of painting," that is to say an understanding which is both alienated and investigative of what there is in the world, right up to the furthermost limit which astounded his contemporaries. The whole of his creative thought involved an Intellect which observed from an alienated point of view, which looked with attention. He was, in other words, a painter who had reached such heights of folly that he could not possibly have been limited by painting or art in general and who was, indeed, obliged not to be an artist. Art was not bestowed upon him, it was perceived by insight. Leonardo was the greatest artistic project of the Renaissance.
(L.M. Batkin, *Leonardo da Vinci*, 1988)

1

1. Arno Landscape, *1473, pen and brown ink and wash on paper, 19.6 × 28 cm. Gabinetto dei disegni e delle stampe degli Uffizi, Florence. The inscription in the artist's hand in the margin of the sheet allows us to date this drawing 5 August 1473, so that it is considered to be the oldest dated work by Leonardo. The work is extraordinarily innovatory for the period, above all because it depicts a real location rather than an unspecified landscape, and also because of the particular way the artist represents nature. This is observed with unprecedented perceptiveness and recreated on paper by means of dynamic pen strokes which immediately depict the world as it really is, no longer forming outlines, but creating a closely-woven network of vibrating lines, which build up a spatial dimension composed of atmosphere, air and light.*

2

2, 3. Andrea Verrocchio and
Leonardo da Vinci, Baptism
of Christ, c. 1472-1475, panel,
177 × 151 cm. Galleria degli Uffizi,
Florence.
This painting was executed by
Verrocchio for the church of San Salvi
in Florence. According to the oldest
sources, the face of the angel on the
left, with its blurred outlines and
delicate sfumato, was by the hand of
the pupil. However, more recently it
has been thought that Leonardo was
also responsible for the left part of the
landscape in the background, a steep-
sided valley along which flows a river
that in the foreground reflects the light
shining from above. Scholars have
come to this conclusion as a result of a
stylistic examination and X-ray
analysis which have ascertained that
the angel's face and Christ's hair, as
well as some parts of the landscape in
the background, were completed in oils
over a ground prepared with tempera.

4

4. Annunciation, c. 1474, panel, 104 × 217 cm. Galleria degli Uffizi, Florence.

Coming from the church of San Bartolomeo di Monteoliveto, the panel was for a long time thought to be by Domenico Ghirlandaio. The attribution to the young Leonardo dates back to the second half of the last century and caused perplexity on the part of many scholars. But in the light of the most recent studies of the different stages of Leonardo's activity as a painter, it seems to have been fully confirmed. The archangel, kneeling on a carpet of meticulously painted flowers, is perhaps the most successful part of the painting; the drapery which he is wearing, especially the sleeve, displays a marvellous eye for colour and composition. In the distance, beyond a row of trees with their varied silhouettes, can be seen, wrapped in the clear dawn light, a landscape with a small town overlooking a bay dotted with ships.

5

5. Study for the Sleeve of the
Angel in the Annunciation,
c. 1474, red chalk, 8.5 × 9.5 cm.
Christ Church, Oxford.

6

6. Ginevra de' Benci, *c. 1474, panel, 42 × 37 cm. National Gallery, of Art, Washington. The panel, which is painted on both sides, depicts on the front, according to sixteenth century sources, the noblewoman Ginevra de' Benci,* daughter of the Florentine banker Amerigo de' Benci, with whom Leonardo was on friendly terms. The girl's name is alluded to by the sprig of juniper encircled by a palm frond and laurel branch which appears on the reverse of the panel. *Since this wreath is truncated at the base, it can be assumed that about a third of the painting has been cut off. It is possible that the lower part of the painting, in which the hands were represented, was never brought to completion.*

7

7. Virgin with the Flowers, *1475-1478, panel, 62 × 47 cm. Alte Pinakothek, Munich.*
The painting is one of Leonardo's early works; in fact, the links with Verrocchio are still evident. Besides, a number of stylistic features recall the Madonna in the Annunciation *in the Uffizi (Plate 4). The figure of the Virgin and Child rises in the pictorial space with its imposing structure, while their ample forms are stressed by the light from the front which illuminates the Virgin's face and shows up the small folds in the edges*

of her robe. The complex interplay of composition and colour in the drapery, the precisely-painted details of the Virgin's plaited hair and a number of stylistic refinements lend a stately, even sumptuous, tone to the scene.

8. Benois Madonna, *c. 1478, panel, 48 × 31 cm. Hermitage, Leningrad.*
Painted shortly after the Virgin with the Flowers *(Plate 7), it is the work which is most probably one of those referred to in the inscription by Leonardo on a drawing in the Uffizi, according to which in 1478 he began*

to paint "the two pictures of the Virgin Mary." Previously attributed to Verrocchio and Lorenzo di Credi, the painting has a number of minor lacunas and has been repainted as a result of past restoration. Compared with the Virgin with the Flowers, *to which it is linked from an iconographic point of view, the painting displays, through the gestures and the exchange of glances of the two protagonists, an intimate relationship which up to that time had been unthinkable in painting of the Quattrocento.*

9

9. Study for the Adoration
of the Magi, *c. 1481, pen and ink,
wash and white heightening,
16.3 × 29 cm. Gabinetto dei disegni
e delle stampe degli Uffizi, Florence.
This is one of the many studies and
preparatory drawings which Leonardo*
executed for the Adoration of the
Magi *(Plate 10). Unlike the final
composition, which was never
completed, this work is still an attempt
to define, in terms of geometry and
perspective, the space intended to
contain the figures. The magnificent*
*architectural motive, visible through
the closely-woven network of lines, was
then surpassed by the Uffizi picture.
Here "atmospheric" space was
dominant, created by the density of
the air, by the effects of light and by
the very movement of the figures.*

10

10. Adoration of the Magi, *1481-1482, "giallolino" and bistre on panel, 246 × 243 cm. Galleria degli Uffizi, Florence.*
In 1481 the monks of San Donato a Scopeto, near Florence, commissioned Leonardo to paint an altarpiece representing the Adoration of the Magi. In fact, this was the only well-documented commission of Leonardo's early Florentine period and the first one in which the artist was engaged on a great work of art. The work is unfinished, with only the underdrawing visible; despite this, besides the simple drawing in green earth, the images are also given life by the application of chiaroscuro with subtle tonal gradations. Leonardo never delivered the work to the monks at Scopeto; in 1496 they replaced it with a painting by Filippino Lippi of the same subject. At present the splendid composition is marred by the presence of a large number of flaws which ought to be removed through cleaning and conservation.

11

11. Saint Jerome, *1481-1482, panel,*
103 × 75 cm. Pinacoteca Vaticana,
Rome.
Despite the lack of documentary
evidence or preliminary drawings
which allow this work to be associated
with Leonardo, there have never been
doubts concerning its attribution, and
this is fully confirmed by analysis of
both technique and style. The recent
restoration of the painting, which
never got beyond the monochrome
stage, has ascertained the existence
of traces of past repainting.

12

12, 13. Virgin of the Rocks
(Madonna with Child, the Infant
Saint John and an Angel), *c. 1483-
1490, panel transferred to canvas,
198 × 122 cm. Louvre, Paris.
The composition, which was
transferred to canvas at the end of the
eighteenth century, introduced new*
*iconographic and stylistic concepts
to Milan that were to bring about
profound changes in the Lombard
painting of the period. Leonardo
substituted an involved composition,
centring on a precise iconographic
and symbolic relationship, for the
traditional image of the Madonna*
*on a throne holding the Child in her
arms. The figures, which form a
pyramidal structure, are set in a rocky
landscape at the entrance to a cave—
the symbol of the mystery and obscurity
of nature—in which the almost
palpable atmosphere of humid
luminosity can be felt to thicken.*

14

14-16. Virgin of the Rocks (Madonna with Child, the Infant Saint John and an Angel), *c. 1495-1508, panel, 189.5 × 120 cm. National Gallery, London.*
The painting, which was painted with the collaboration of his pupil Giovanni Ambrogio de' Predis, was probably executed to substitute the original work, which was perhaps never delivered to the Confraternity and consequently not displayed in San Francesco Grande. The London painting presents an intentional simplification of the involved iconographic and symbolic contents of the Paris version, while, stylistically, the figures are endowed with greater solidity and are more imposing, their lineaments accentuated by greater use of chiaroscuro and the cooler tones of his palette. The greater intensity of the shadows, together with a somewhat less meticulous attention to detail, also characterise the immediate surroundings and the distant landscape in the background.

17

17. Portrait of a Musician, 1485-1490, panel, 44 × 32 cm. Pinacoteca Ambrosiana, Milan. The painting, which is the only male portrait on a panel which can be attributed to Leonardo, dates from the early years of the artist's stay in Milan. While the hair and the face, with their warm tonality of colour, are painted in very great detail and display an extraordinary degree of skill, the robe, the stole and the hand with the scroll definitely seem to be unfinished. The removal, at the beginning of this century, of repainting from the lower part of the painting led to the discovery of the right hand holding a scroll on which there are staves, musical notes and a number of faded letters. The attempts to identify the sitter have, therefore, focused on the most prominent musicians of the Milanese court, in particular Franchino Gaffurio and the Flemish composer Josquin des Pres, but it has not been possible to come to a definite conclusion.

18

18, 19. Lady with an Ermine (Portrait of Cecilia Gallerani?), *c. 1490, panel, 54 × 40 cm. Czartoryski Muzeum, Cracow. The young woman has been almost unanimously identified by scholars as Cecilia Gallerani, Ludovico il Moro's cultured and refined mistress. There is a reference to her surname in the* *Greek name for ermine, which was a symbol of purity and chastity. Despite the fact that some parts are unfinished and others are repainted—especially the background, the outlines and the hair—this portrait must certainly be considered as one of the artist's finest paintings. The great skill with which Leonardo resolved the problem of the* *dynamics of the human body in space, the intense psychological introspection of the face, the vivacious expression of the eyes, together with an elegantly refined appearance, make this painting one of the great masterpieces, not only of Leonardo's oeuvre, but also of Renaissance portraiture in general.*

20

20, 21. La Belle Ferronnière,
c. 1495-1499, panel, 62 × 44 cm.
Louvre, Paris.
In the past there has been considerable
controversy regarding the attribution
to Leonardo of the portrait of a lady
known as "La Belle Ferronnière."
Now, however, with only a few
exceptions, scholars tend to ascribe this
painting to the artist because of the
evident similarities of style and
subject-matter—the dark background,
the diagonal positioning of the bust,
the body which seems to revolve in
space, the intense expression of the
eyes—that it has in common with the
other two portraits which he executed
during his first stay in Milan.
The numerous attempts to identify the
sitter have not so far been able to
produce adequate documentary
evidence or find confirmation of an
iconographic nature. The hypothesis
which has gained the greatest credit
among scholarly opinion is that the
woman is none other than Cecilia
Gallerani who was portrayed by
Leonardo, only a few years previously,
in the painting now in Cracow (Plates
18, 19).

22

22-24. Last Supper, *1495-1497, tempera and oil on two layers of* intonaco, *460 × 880 cm. Refectory, Santa Maria delle Grazie, Milan. Leonardo interpreted the subject in a wholly innovatory manner, depicting the moment of greatest dramatic tension in the narration of the Gospels: the announcement of His imminent betrayal by Christ, who is isolated at the centre of the scene, and the agitated reaction of the Apostles who question each other incredulously, displaying consternation and astonishment. The brilliant way the composition was structured, thanks to the adoption of an experimental pictorial technique, should have constituted, from Leonardo's point of view, the stylistic embodiment of his research into the inner recesses of the human spirit, thus representing the very essence of his artistic tenets. While his refusal to adopt the fresco technique allowed the artist to give finishing touches, make improvements and "veil" the figures, in order to confer "spirit and breath" on them, the pigments—bound with tempera or oily substances on very thin layers of intonaco—proved to be extremely vulnerable to humidity and the effects of external agents. Already in the second half of the sixteenth century a number of sources refer to the poor state of conservation of the painting. Since then, over the centuries, there have been numerous attempts at restoration, some of them involving additions or repainting. As can be seen in Plate 24, the most recent one discovered under the repainting images which, even if they offer only a faint trace of the originals, appear to be endowed with a luminosity and purity of colour which was quite unexpected.*

25

25. Portrait of Isabella d'Este, *c. 1500, black chalk and pastel on paper, 63 × 46 cm. Louvre, Paris. The drawing, which was executed on paper in black and red chalk, is at present in a poor state of conservation. The flesh, especially around the lineaments of the face, is delicately modelled with shades of pink which,* with slightly darker tones, are also to be found in the hair. The folds, the voile and the ribbons which are part of the woman's dress are, on the other hand, faintly drawn with touches of yellow. Along the lines which give shape to Isabella's magnificent dress and define the right hand are still visible the minute pinpricks which were intended to allow very fine charcoal powder to filter through to the surface of the painting so that it could reproduce the outline. Despite insistent requests, Leonardo never completed the portrait of the Mantuan noblewoman, just limiting himself to lightly going over in ink the profile and the outline of the hair.

26

26. Study for the Head of Leda,
1506-1507, pen and ink, 35 × 20 cm.
Civiche Raccolte d'Arte al Castello
Sforzesco, Milan.
Leda, the mythical Greek heroine was
the subject of a painting to which
Leonardo dedicated himself during his
second stay in Florence. The drawing
emphasizes the extent of the artist's

interest in women's hairstyles,
something he had inherited from
Verrocchio. Here he depicts Leda's
hair with truly surprising complexity
and a high aesthetic level. All that
remains of the painting are some
invaluable descriptions, a large
number of copies and a few sketches
by the artist. These allow us, however,

not only to follow the stylistic evolution
of the theme in Leonardo's mind—
from the kneeling version to the
standing one—but also to recognise in
the original picture the first example
of a type of drawing, the so-called
"serpentine figure," which was
extremely popular in the sixteenth
century.

28

27. The Virgin and Child
with Saint Anne, *1499-1508?,*
light ochre, charcoal, tempera and
white heightening, 159 × 101 cm.
National Gallery, London.
This cartoon in the National Gallery
and the one depicting the Portrait
of Isabella d'Este *(Plate 25) are the*
only cartoons which survive out of the
large number which Leonardo
prepared for his paintings. Scholars,

in fact, tend to to place the work in the
period from 1499, the last year of
Leonardo's stay in Milan, to around
1508, the year in which, after his stay
in Florence, he returned to the
Lombard city. Thanks to the
harmonious composition of the forms
and the restrained lyricism of its
emotional content, this picture must be
considered one of the most sublime
expressions of Leonardo's art.

28. Study for the Virgin and
Child with Saint Anne, *c. 1510-*
1513, pen and ink and charcoal
on paper, 12.5 × 10 cm. Gallerie
dell'Accademia, Venice.

29

29, 30. The Virgin and Child
with Saint Anne, *c. 1510-1513,
panel, 168 × 122 cm. Louvre, Paris.
Although this painting—which was
probably executed during Leonardo's
second stay in Milan—is unfinished
and partly repainted, it is the final
version of the theme which he had
already dealt with in a previous
cartoon, since lost, and in the*
*composition now in the National
Gallery in London. The pyramidal
construction of the group is perfectly
balanced, with Saint Anne at the
apex, glancing towards the Virgin.
She, in her turn, leans down and
stretches out her arms towards her son
who, embracing a lamb, repeats his
mother's affectionate gesture. It is,
therefore, through the contemplative*
*intimacy of this family scene, pervaded
by a wonderful atmosphere of
peacefulness, that the theme of the
Incarnation of Christ is expressed in
allegorical form. Behind the group,
there is a fantastic vista of mountain
peaks, glaciers and watery wastes,
wrapped in icy mists and frozen in an
atmosphere of impenetrable silence
where time has ceased to exist.*

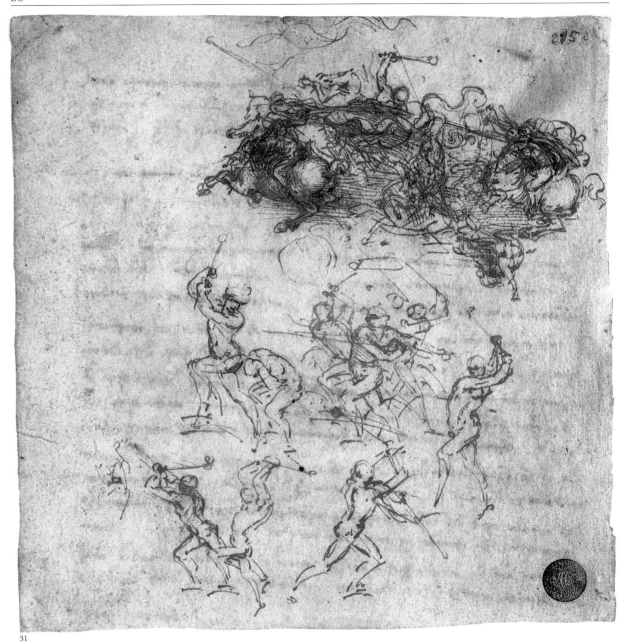

31. Study for the Battle of
Anghiari, Skirmishes between
Horsemen and Foot Soldiers,
1504, pen and ink on paper,
16.5 × 15.3 cm. Gallerie
dell'Accademia, Venice.

32

32. Head of a Warrior, c. 1504,
chalk, 19.2 × 18.8 cm. Szépmüvészeti
Muzeum, Budapest.
*This famous head of a warrior, which
was drawn on the verso of a sheet in
the national museum in Budapest, is
one of the very few drawings by
Leonardo which almost certainly refer
to the battle of Anghiari. The recto of
the sheet depicts, instead, the profile of*
*another head of a warrior, which,
however, does not display the expressive
intensity of the first drawing. Through
the dramatic incisiveness of the warrior
and the attention given to the details of
the face, this analytical study already
gives a clear idea of the violent twisting
of the bodies and the extreme tension of
the composition present in the whole
work.*

33

33. Bacchus, *1511-1513, canvas,*
177 × 115 cm. Louvre, Paris.
Originally the painting represented
Saint John the Baptist in the desert,
but in the second half of the
seventeenth century it was
transformed, with additions and
modifications, into the god Bacchus.
Because this radically altered its
nature, the painting can neither be
considered to form part of the artist's
oeuvre nor to be a significant example
of the new aesthetic concept which
Leonardo had developed in that
period.

34. Saint John the Baptist, *1513-*
1516, panel, 69 × 57 cm. Louvre,
Paris.
The painting was probably executed
during the last years of Leonardo's
stay in Rome, and is wholly by his
hand. The figure who is depicted,
wrapped in a soft all-embracing
shadow, displays that expression
of languid ambiguity which was so
typical of the artist's last portraits. In
the case of this work the use of sfumato
is excessive, giving the whole image a
somewhat ungainly appearance.

35

36

35, 36. Mona Lisa, *1503-1506/ 1513, panel, 77 × 53 cm. Louvre, Paris.*
Since Giorgio Vasari's story that the woman portrayed by Leonardo was Mona Lisa, wife of the Florentine merchant Francesco del Giocondo, has proved to be unreliable, the identity of the "Lady on the Balcony," one of the all-time masterpieces of art history, is still a topic of scholarly dispute. The

problem is, however, of minor importance compared with the great artistic merits of the painting, which is an unprecedented work in the field of portraiture thanks to the naturalness of the figure's pose, the extreme softness of the drapery, the barely perceptible translucency of the veils which cover her figure and the complexity of the psychological nuances which animate the

indefinable expression of her face. The extraordinary tonal and stylistic unity of the painting, the sense of being in a "timeless" dimension which both figure and landscape emanate, are also due to the effect of the layers of paint, which as well as having a vital protective function, tone down and render more uniform the luminosity, intensity and transparency of Leonardo's original colours.

37

37. *Deluge, c. 1516, black chalk, pen
and ink on paper, 16.2 × 20.3 cm.
Royal Library, Windsor Castle.*
*This work, which was executed in
black chalk with touches of yellowish
ink, forms part of a series of sixteen
drawings dealing with the theme of the
Deluge. This terrible apocalyptic
vision, dating from the last years of*
*the artist's life, in which all the forces
of nature are unleashed with
appallingly destructive violence in a
catastrophe which obliterates the
presence of man, became a concrete
expression of Leonardo's extremely
dramatic meditation on the universe
and all the constituent parts of
creation.*

Essential Bibliography

L'opera completa di Leonardo pittore, edited by A. Ottino della Chiesa, Milan 1967.

C. Pedretti, *Leonardo. A Study in Chronology and Style*, London 1973.

A. M. Brizio, "Leonardo pittore," in *Leonardo*, edited by L. Reti, Milan 1974.

Leonardo. La pittura, Florence 1977, 2nd ed. 1985.

Leonardo da Vinci, Disegni anatomici della Biblioteca Reale di Windsor, catalogue of the exhibition, Palazzo Vecchio, Florence 1979.

C. Pedretti, *Leonardo*, Bologna 1979.

M. Rosci, *Leonardo*, Milan 1979.

S. J. Freedberg, *The Pelican History of Art, Painting in Italy 1500-1600*, Harmondsworth, Middlesex, 1979.

Leonardo da Vinci–Nature Studies from the Royal Library at Windsor Castle, catalogue of the exhibition by Carlo Pedretti, introduction by Kenneth Clark, 1981, Royal Academy of Arts, London.

Leonardo da Vinci–The Codex Hammer formerly the Codex Leicester, catalogue of the exhibition by Jane Roberts, introduction by Carlo Pedretti, 1981, Royal Academy of Arts, London.

Leonardo e l'età della ragione, edited by E. Bellone and P. Rossi, Milan 1982.

Leonardo e Milano, edited by G.A. Dell'Acqua, Milan 1982.

Frederick Hartt, *History of Italian Renaissance Art*, London 1987.

Leonardo scomparso e ritrovato, catalogue of the exhibition, Palazzo Medici Riccardi, Florence 1988.

L. M. Batkin, *Leonardo da Vinci*, Bari 1988.

Leonardo da Vinci, catalogue of the exhibition, Hayward Gallery, London 1989.

P. C. Marani, *Leonardo e i leonardeschi nei musei della Lombardia*, Milan 1990.

Printed for Arnoldo Mondadori Arte
by Fantonigrafica - Elemond Editori Associati